Hugo And Splot

Written by Frank Pedersen

Illustrated by Graeme Tavendale

Contents	Page
Chapter 1. *Two old friends meet*	4
Chapter 2. *A Nile River adventure*	13
Chapter 3. *Tiring adventures*	18
Chapter 4. *An icy adventure*	24
Chapter 5. *The end of the holiday*	28
Verse	32

Rigby

Hugo And Splot

With these characters ...

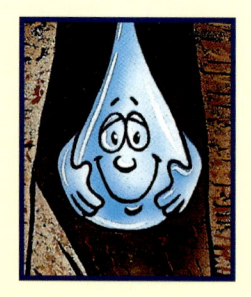

Hugo

Splot

"Water cycle

Setting the scene ...

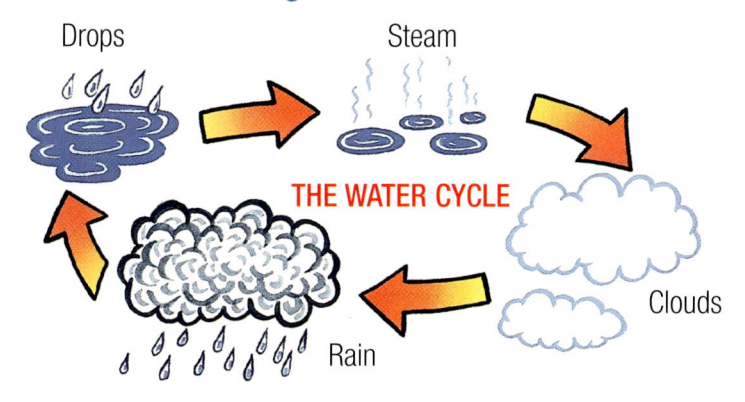

Drops Steam

THE WATER CYCLE

Clouds

Rain

Hugo and his friend Splot are water droplets. Kept apart for millions of years, they meet again on the roof of a cave. They tell each other about some of the adventures they have had.

Throughout the years, they both shared the same water cycle. First they were drops of water; then they evaporated and became steam; then they became clouds; then they condensed and rained down as water again. But they both ended up in some very interesting places!

adventures never end ..."

Chapter 1.

Deep within a dark, damp cave, Hugo the water droplet was on vacation. He hung from the roof of the cave. Beneath him, a stream trickled out into the daylight.

Every few minutes, droplets from other parts of the cave roof dripped into the stream. When Hugo's vacation was over, he too would drip off the roof and into the stream.

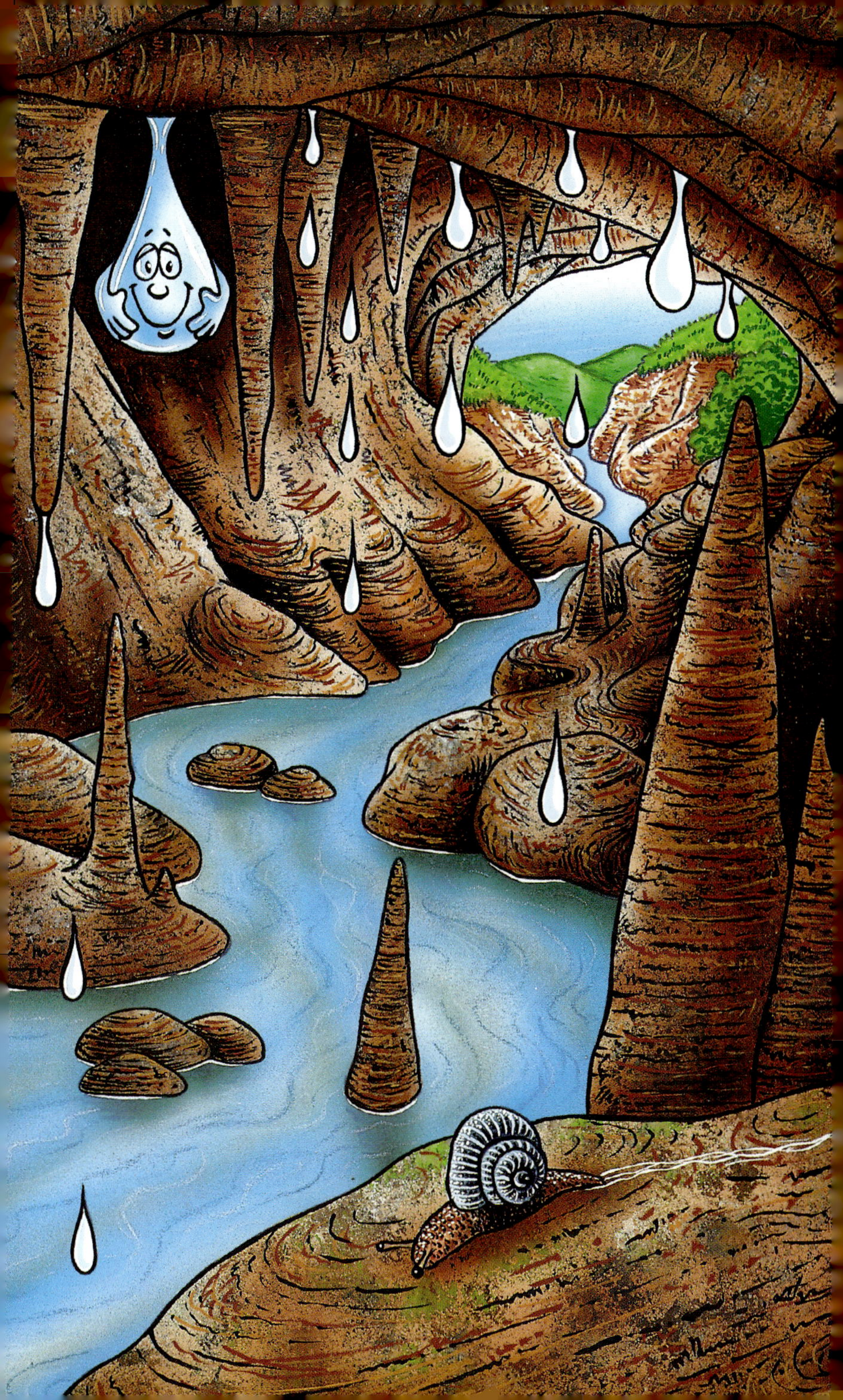

Suddenly, Hugo heard something other than drips and trickles.

"Hey! Hugo! Is that you?"

Hugo looked around. Where was the voice coming from?

"Hey! Hugo! Over here!"

Hugo swirled around in surprise. He almost dropped off the roof.

"Splot! What are you doing here?"

"I'm on vacation, just like you," replied Splot. "I haven't seen you since the dinosaur adventure."

Splot and Hugo were old friends. They hadn't seen each other for millions of years. The last time they saw each other, they had shared a puddle — until they were slurped up by a thirsty dinosaur.

Hugo remembered being in the dinosaur's stomach, surrounded by smelly bits of food. He and Splot had sloshed from side to side as the dinosaur walked.

9

Slowly the water droplets in the dinosaur's stomach became separated. Some, like Splot, went into the dinosaur's blood.

"After I went into the dinosaur's blood, where did you end up?" Splot asked. Hugo frowned at him.

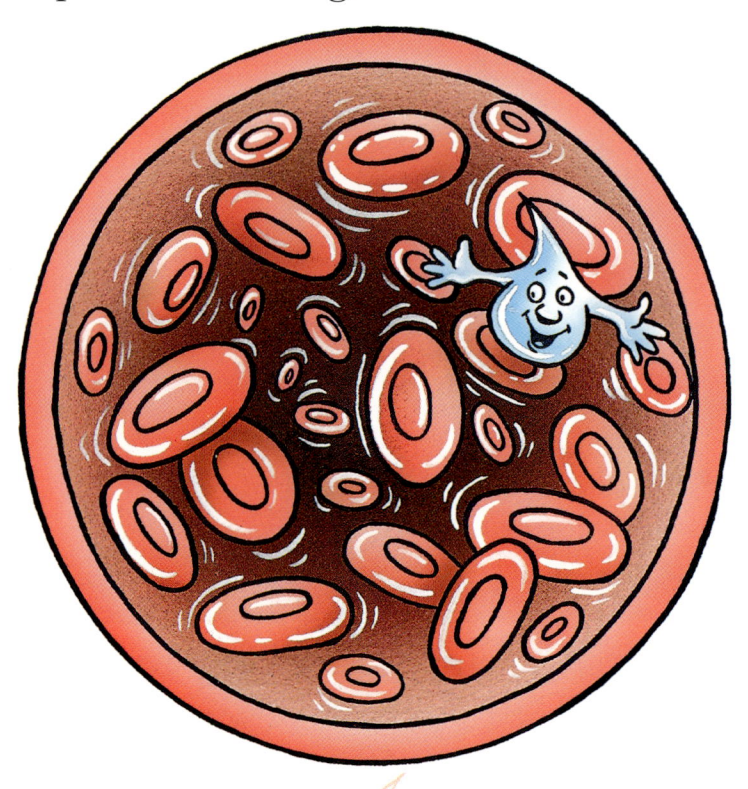

"That dinosaur got rid of me into another puddle!"

"The sun's heat turned me and the other puddle droplets into steam. The steam rose, and we became a cloud."

"That's still better than what happened to me," said Splot. He made a face. "Our dinosaur wasn't very smart. It fell into a swamp. Before I knew what was happening, I was covered in mud, sand, and stones. It took me weeks to find my way out."

Chapter 2.

Now it was Hugo's turn to tell his friend about his Nile River adventure.

"Once, a few friends and I dropped into a long, wide river called the Nile. Each day, more raindrops fell into the river, until there were enough of us to flood over the land," began Hugo.

"Then what happened?" asked Splot.

"The soil we carried along with us made the land fertile. People who lived along the Nile were able to grow things in fertile soil. I ended up in a wheat plant. Then my wheat plant was used to make a loaf of bread," said Hugo.

"Soon, I was in a hungry person's mouth, down their throat, and into their stomach. I stayed inside that body for longer than in our dinosaur!"

"One day, that person's body became very warm. So warm that my droplet friends and I came out through the person's skin. We formed drops of sweat on that person's face. Then, I looked around."

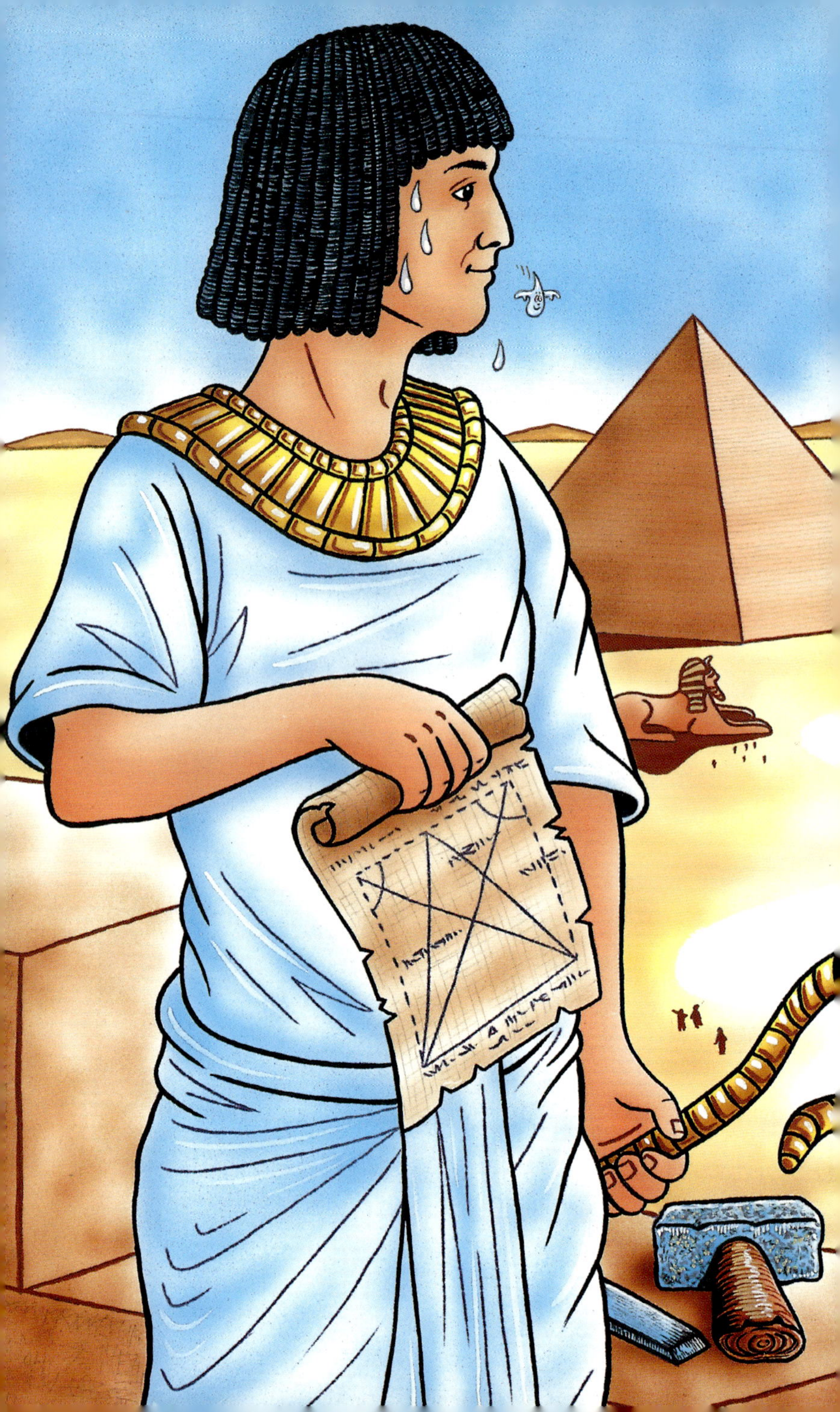

"There I was on top of a tall pyramid in the hot desert! Our person had been helping to build a pyramid in the hot sun. Soon, the sun's heat made us evaporate again, and up we floated!"

"It's always the same," Splot said, nodding. "Drop down into one place, float off to another. Our water cycle adventures never end."

Chapter 3.

Splot told Hugo about his most enjoyable and his least enjoyable adventures. Splot's most enjoyable adventure was when he had been swirled and swooshed around to make a bubble bath.

His least enjoyable adventure was when he had been used to wash up piles of dirty dishes. He was drained away into smelly drains and sewers. Yuck!

"What was your most tiring adventure?" asked Splot.

"My most tiring adventure was about a hundred years ago," said Hugo. "I was sitting quietly on a barrel of water. Just then, a noisy steam train rumbled up beside me."

"We were poured from the barrel into the steam engine. Suddenly, we were moving and shaking about. We were getting hotter. The fire made our water bubble and boil. We turned into steam. The steam started to move the wheels of the train," said Hugo.

"Just when I thought I couldn't take any more, I was free. I left the steam engine with a loud whistling sound. Phew! I was glad to get out of there! That was my most tiring adventure."

Hugo's story reminded Splot of his sad iceberg adventure in 1912. Splot dribbled into a more comfortable spot before he told Hugo what had happened.

Chapter 4.

"Hundreds of years ago, before my sad iceberg adventure, I was in a cloud. My cloud was blown so far north, I froze. Instead of falling as rain, I fell to the ground as snow," said Splot.

"Layers and layers of snow fell on top of me. Slowly, I was squeezed into the biggest iceblock you've ever seen. We became a frozen river of ice called a glacier. We slid downhill."

"Just when I was enjoying the nice slide, another block of ice fell away in front of us. Our glacier had slid to the edge of the sea! With a roar, our block of ice broke off. We fell into the icy seawater and floated away. We had become an iceberg."

"One night in 1912, we were floating in the sea. Suddenly, a steamship came speeding towards our iceberg. What a shock," said Splot.

"We hoped the steamship would miss our iceberg. But it was too late. It crashed into us. That *really* was a sad night."

Tears dribbled from Splot's eyes.

"I heard about that disaster," said Hugo. "It sounded really horrible."

Chapter 5.

After many days, the two water droplets had talked about all their adventures. Now their holiday had to end.

"I'm dripping off into the stream tonight," said Splot sadly. "My holidays never last long enough!"

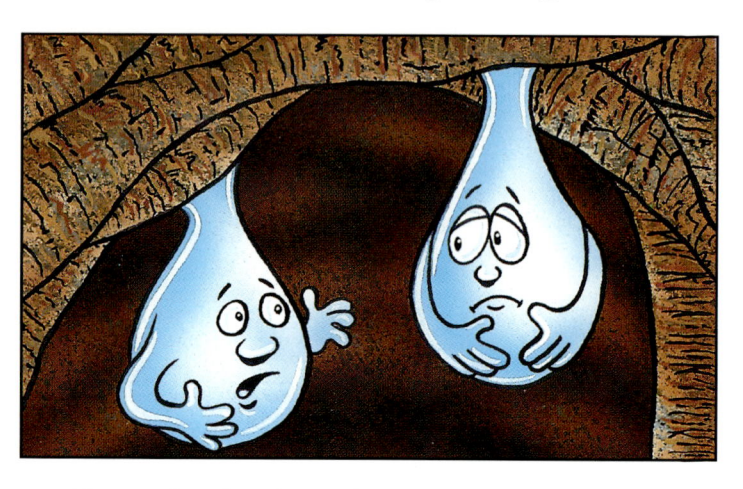

Hugo looked sad that his friend was leaving. He knew it might be another 60 million years before they met again.

"I have to drop down into the stream when the sun comes up tomorrow," said Hugo. "Back to work for me too!"

"By the time you leave, the stream will have carried me far away. I might have been drunk, dribbled, dripped, drizzled, and dried," laughed Splot.

That night, Splot waved goodbye to Hugo. He began to dribble down a stalactite. At the bottom, he waited for more droplets.

A ball of water grew at the end of the stalactite. It grew until the water droplets could hold on no more.

"See you next t-i-i-i-i-m-e!"

Hugo heard Splot's voice fading away. Far below, he heard a tiny splash.

Alone, Hugo tried to enjoy the last hours of his holiday. Starting tomorrow, he would have a lot of work to do, so he would not be bored.

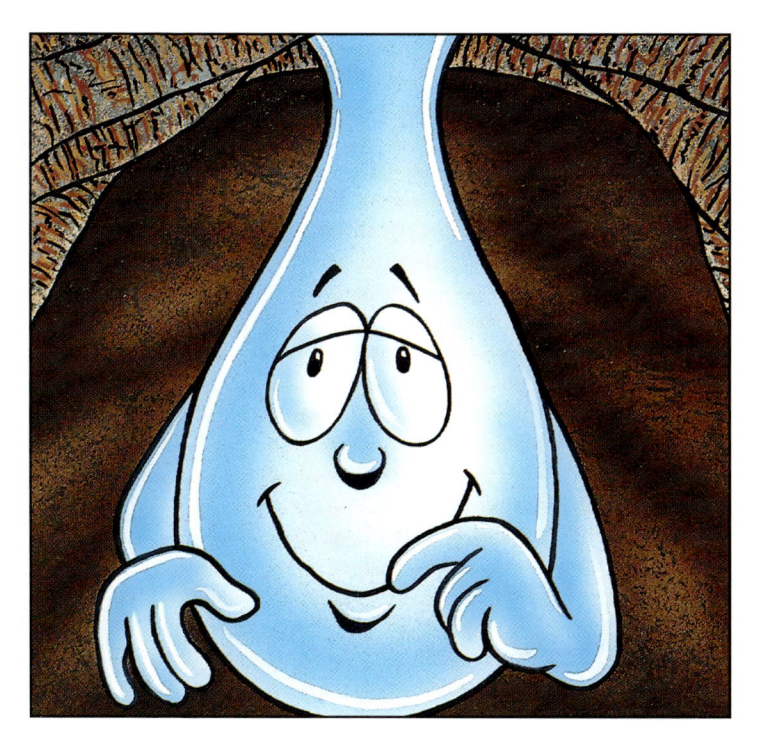

With so many streams, rivers, lakes, oceans, clouds, glaciers, and icebergs out there, life as a water droplet was *never* boring!

"Rain and Shine"

Water droplets keep moving
All the time
Through an
Endless cycle of
Rain and shine.